life-list

life-list

Jessica Smith

chax
2015

chax / po box 162 / victoria tx 77902-0162 / usa

Life-List
ISBN 978-0-9862640-2-3

Art work on the cover:
Albrecht Dürer, 1512, *Wing of a European Roller*, or *Flügel einer Blaurake*.
The digital image file we have used is in the public domain and "free of
known restrictions under copyright law, including all related and neighboring
rights," in the U.S., according to Wikipedia Commons. The original art work
is currently in the possession of the Albertina Museum, Vienna, Austria.

Chax Press is currently located at the University of Houston Victoria Center
for the Arts, in downtown Victoria, Texas. We thank the University, and
particularly the School of Arts & Sciences, for its support. We also wish to
thank interns who are helping our work in the Spring of 2015: Georgette
Walker, Enkeleta Dervishi, Drenica Dervishi, Melissa Cluff, and Laura Hicks.

for the coven

1. observation

2. memory

Reside in possibilities of meaning.
Robert Grenier

hero

       n

every day

s   till

stand   ing

still

in   the same place,

      same   stalky   l   eggs

                      rooted

like a tall water-   plant

great   blue-   grey

solitary sandpiper

pipes

      peeps

            dying

      d

           bobs with his head,   skids

           into the water

f lies like a sw allow

      lost   as   he

swal lows

           lands
bobs abo ve the
           water
           water

      alpine

      wate r

           ead
           lake

           next to me,
           i drink from his
           water

everyear,

re terns

statue by the shoreline   very ear

sit   s   t

ing

read: listening for frogs

i ll   know where to find   for   og   s
you

d

for age

line   back to

knowhere

meet

great blue concrete   rookery

reed   t

he

return

cryptic coloration

rich   echoes
downward

spiral   through

                                             e

the deepening gloom

                         loom   v   ery

uni form cinnamon   threaded note-
                 forest   web   ethereal

                           descending *whew*
                   relief
             in the gloaming

make a little house and stop working

Japanese beetle

and no birds sing

songbirds were
sac   ing # of dead and
                                                                      dying

                                             it was   birds

could not fly
it continued to   rificed

                                    alarm   even words
    les fly

          beat its wings and clutch

                                          with the   tremoring loss
                                          birds.
                                                  brown thrashers, starlings,
                      loss of ability to fly, paralysis, convulsions   meadow

                                                        its beak

                                                                          ts side

                ficial been changed   larks, grac was held
                with its toes   lying
                      and breathing was labored
  the once
                rain had   open

          bene

loon/lune

a

high-pitched

thin
chin   loud   whales
strap

laugh   acid

(wailing) red-throated   and shrieks

rain

mourn-   lakes where these had   bred

grebes dive expertly

sterilized

ful

many

sus   yodel   oil

bulky   ceptible

mass

spills

to

18

swim

un

at

rising under hills
    s cene
    water a   sometimes rapidly
    ways

b

   to   pace

rivers

y

so   dark subsurface sea

c

always on the move,

closed   r
separate

su

sinking beneath valleys.

wells

m   p a n son

ped   slow to

is

tap

ca/co

:herons

c

migratory

catalyzing air

:pelicans

l   ear   paths

and

lake

:grebes

sunlight

drifting ribbons

:gulls

he

ck   of

a   fun

small as dust

nel

blue-eyed grass

                    soft needles   glacial pathways

                               from

number: moraine

               drips

shadow

sun night.   larches

moon day.

patterns mountain time.

                            with   different kinds:

motion tree time.

crossings flower time.

                            waxy   watches

time-fabric

     every day, flowers

     anew   soft   seasons

                         needles

listen

thrush

                                                        is

                                not

                spiral   tumb

                ing   ard

                        cracking
                        calving
                        the first shard   le
fugue   clashes against
                        the next
                        falling thousands
                        upon thousands
                        the noise of mountains
                                        down
        he   wards like

                unseen but

hermit of the   pebbles on
trees, hides   pebbles

            from us listening to the

                                        mtns

22

messaien

t

   s

      the birds together   down

                    ha

                plant

                   ve

o nce in the   morning and
then the   chorus only   of
all day long   l azier   un
                             hoar ser
                             by
                             comp   air   ison

         cup

                                flanks

     a

           n me   rufus

                        is   to   b

husk   y   *chick-a-dee-dee*

                        natural cavity

     moss   in a
     i er   ior of   dense sp   ces
                              ru

        nt   a

hermit

rootlets / spiraling

ca

ll

clear
/ phrases

note

stands tall

concealed /
musical

a low

reedy tremolo   vol

increases as
one closes in

tuck

slice

grub   slow

cater

it was, therefore, it could be
other wise.

continuous screw

life from the life,   `ea

feeding   durational

`e   pillar

turn
worm

new leaves

a`u   new dead

en   un ear th-

leaves

span,

p

we are consequently

links

lover

das lied von der erde

pale   strata

    a teaspoon of topsoil

                      are?

                                                  constant change--

           th

    cranberry bog,
    strawberry root weevil

                                   like

        read-

                                filaments

                macerate *chomp chomp*
patch   work   covering   works its creative magic
within the fallen needles

                                minute

    primitive wingless insects called *springtails*

                                ceaseless

                                cycles

water skeleton

                    ear

                th/   heard   of
                    c
                waves / brea   st   s
                                                          ark
                                                    i
(assert the generative)
                              king
                                                    blue amputated
                                                    limbs
                                                    nonhand
                                                    hanging clustered /
                                          grotesque hybirds

                                    ice berg
                        ttered   i   bex
                                                          crypt-throated

        l   only   sha

                              drilled/   tin   fissures

                              dancing of home

silence any song

what to   a diminished thing

                                                    pill

mid-   summer is   to

                              spring

                   thrush music—hark!

                                              as   one two

                        make of   ten

air died

too   a   cry

          in

           the breath of   stal chill

dark in the woods

                                        cold

                                                  r

                                    shoe

                  no bird was singing in it now

          dark   n't

for a bird

                  would

                                      d

he knows   singing not to sing

conspicuous eater

chiefly mature

br   / repetitive

il li

hurried
burry

woodland / warbler   t
call note
call
                              an

gleams in the sunlight
                              scarlet   w/
patch   work   plum   age   while

chip-bang
                                        ing
black win   molt
                        gs   and   tale

king fisher

lavender's

    a lichen form   that stares

                          blue

    green   wounded and wasted,

      blue   blue

penetrating   lavender's

rattle   dagger-like   *roi pêscheur*

   blue

      conspicuously crested

           green

           too big for a house, he

lavender's   digs into earthen banks to lay eggs

   blue   green

        bill   *kleck*

     -gray

thumb-sucking knowledge

                      blue

     green

raven

                                                           black

                                                           curls

               aerial displays

                                                                 wisps the
                                                                 black b lends
                                                                 out

                                   weak and weary

                                                                     dying
                  r   o   ar   a   light

                                                                 golum
                  r   ar   e   cac   k le
                           ar   t   the deep
                                                                     evil;

       he   f e a t h e r
       address   hollow

       places   gutteral croaking   *kraak*

                                                            driven out, poisoned
       trans

                                      p   lance

kites

hideous wings,

grim

lumbering across the sky

ts

in smoke   to high

in

(I fear, I fear!)

heaven

eav

gather locus   ascended

w

gs

to the wall   and without
avail

h   beat
weak

y

res't

broken pods with golden powder

p

us to

forever broken

stuff our gory hearts into their maws

hollow cuckoo

least grebe   earned i
  a series of   t the local

    hollow, c   name "hell-diver"

    uckoo-like notes,
                                                              sel d
cow-cow-cow   *-cow, cow, cow,*

 cowp, cowp, cowp, that
                         that has a black ring around it

slows   om
  advertises its present with   loud, barking calls
down at the end
    stained brown   flyy

    well-hidden flo   *cow-cow-cow-cow,*
                                                                cow, cow,
      cent plants   marsh vegetation

      ating mass of   *cowp, cowp, cowp*

conspicuous buff ear tufts   dead anchored

     to adja   slows down at the end

The Brain—is wider than the sky—
Emily Dickinson

epilogue

escaping, I know

observer on the platform

eyeing every reed
-still
another reed like the rest
easily
bypassed

what to look for

thin tall

brown

hiding among ourselves

builds a flimsy platform

coo-coo-coo

stock

grey early spring

retreat

invisible

blended

in the open marsh
secretive

undercurrents

woven

low in the water,

together   in

dusk on the pink canals
        ribboning through the grain elevators
        solitary, maniacal
                                        some Fate's living room

                        your bird:
                tattooed into your
                        slim pale waist

dark hair falling
smoothly
                        bright contrast of black and white
                        unmistakable

                                we tell each other
                                from the weft

        at night,
                        the bone-hollowing cry
                        "wildest of all wild sounds"

sandhill cranes

bent in the undergrowth   my mockingbirds

              divergent roads:

                               with flat taut tales

from the top of the hand

                     enough to reach

you see   this life in which   fantasies of

   foreign to me,

                   you are lost to me

to the middle of the hand

             and I to you,   the large cold birds

the small warm ones

                  your cranes

a complex duet

                           stained ochre

       laughing purr

    synchronized   migrate south with offspring

      sonogram dunes

           seen in silhouette in the distance

             bring me

              the rare vagrant

to remind me

agelaios

sonic at once

signs

I consider tattooing him
into my skin
virtually any   as a memento

in the tall grass   of water

body

Fort Niagara,
along the water,
chastising

for each clutch

a new nest
the old snows melt,

he follows me
habitat to habitat
a reminder of him

cormorant

later, low

sentinels

stands upright, perched
watchful,   above the water,
in the small motorboat we approach
two islands teeming with   a fast formation
sea birds

in this space their
wings outstretched   painting of a madwoman

does this draw you to them, how

secretly
lost the original

name
planning to stitch their feathers
alone,   into dresses

flowery, even romantic   misremembering

the ascent into madness

Ithaca

a whirlwind

      from the fourth floor
      picture windows   I can kill you;

                you can kill me
  very deeply forked

        vast dancing bodies
        of swallows in accord

    do not adapt themselves
to verbal description

        like leaves

you furtively unhinge
from a house made of doors

              a combination

      deliver a joining
      remove a window-dressing

psychotherapy

extinct

watching breathless
from the window

like a

unable to explain   crow
the possible magic

like a

from afar,
nearly indistinguishable

hurried flicker

a memory of photographs

the one missing,

calculating

a white bill from a distance

alectryomancy

clucking and stamping

                new moon in Aries

not to brood

                    tornado forecast

bred to fight,

gives birth every day

when a pullet becomes a hen,

           summer pattern with squall

her eggs are stolen

          out of pecking order

             reading the omens

breed out the mother   strom brewing over the hills,

          rock foundation of barn

to the side of new houses

hypnotized by threat,

sometimes fly short distances
     to escape previeved danger

          gently shoved to awaken

caged

"retained the ability to make teeth, under certain conditions"

that they did not return

grandfather

generations
finding the same

white-painted gourd clusters
hang in even-numbered
space   sets above the garden

dark black-purple
a language for death   swirls

spoken at

despite the houses

the one who writes and the one who is written

the point of singularity

away

does not go back

passed   through

we hardly see them anymore

the child the

I become

vessel
mother of you

wuthering

        like a bird

                                   migratory
           a hauntology:

                        the path

I called him purple
                          what dreams may

     like a lover
                memory of night
                arms flung out in the
                autumn cool

                extinct
I called him heron
    come   the lips sealed

                    like a ghost

     under how many layers
                  every night
  of earth   flapping against the
                       window

pigeons

smashed   a pair
                                                     against
                                                     the window

                                                                        lost

their way in the snow

                    my boyhood bedroom
                    with frosted winter windows
                    I never had

    a whole life in one moment:

        all the subsequent
                                                loss

                            together

        a borrowed memory:
                                            that

            I arrived to find two silhouettes of doves

piece for sky

rewrite perception

what I discover by walking,   do not harken to nature,

looking up at kerned birds

on powerlines   all this secret information,

does it pertain

what it is like to read   they say, ugly

tag each   *trash bird*

sky-piece:

with a word

everyone

alphabet sequence

a to b   so that they flock in paragraphs

instructions to build   look up and imagine

white concrete cliffs

gone wild in accidental habitat

(not a) dinner party

                                        memory of torn tendons
                                        memory of snapped necks

                              brooding at dinner table
        in the median,

                    death witout chemical byproducts
a Cooper's hawk tears the meat

                    death witout warefare

                              hermit state
the rabbit's meat now
the hawk's meat

                                   threatening war from
              a little boy mouth

        not rich by what we possess but

                    what we can relinquish

king bird

                                        perched, lakeside

                                        shallow water

                    blue-white   atop abstract   metal
                                        waves

tempting in the heat

                         the lake running in
                         five directions
marks his territory

                    kit-kitter

                                   black and white and
                                   the blue-black dragonflies

Lark

her name

                not a bird, but a memory
                of kissing

the sparkle of old memory

what a plunge—

              forged in passionate newness

the plush lips of a sad
romantic telling me,
slow down

rapture of soft skin
found all year long

island of iridescent tree

memory and anticipation:

concrete imbedded with bird footprints

dive-bombing us   their huge circles
unawares   skirting our path

bloody pools of seagull prey

swallows

clear white bellies   swirling
the sky   bright aqua backs

half lake, half rock

each word one of mourning and of hope

feather eddies

not a bird, but an event   wings
it pulls me
in

                                        beyond the pale

                        great blue heron
                        tucked into Amish fields
                                    my own mind
                    the music all night beneath
healing the divide   usual waters
between elation and fear
                        collapsible neck
                        head rests on shoulders

            the light reflects
            trapped under the silver maple grove

a grounded transcendence
                                        tripped

                internal flap of
                giant

robin

a plastic nest hung on

the heat seems to   said *cheer-cheerily*
bleach its   a false tree branch
red   but the long morning song
feathers   persists

        we thought you   in the shade of
    were gone   a sycamore

        the baby open-mouthed,

the pinkish-taupe breast
        and drum of cicadas   signified, foraging

        calling
        for his mother

    pointing, "that

                            in the early green morning
                                in the tent-light
                        I try not to move and disturb
                                your secret song

into the abyss

ivory

  blink-white

                                                      kent, kent

extinct   for others, for other people   a tin trumpet

                                         the one who intends to speak

     buried in a footnote

      if it cannot be found,

                                        but

    "impossible   *a guide to extinct birds*
    inconsolable
    irreconcilable

                     glossily   immobile

from which we have no memory   in photographs

                            resonates,

      follow it

                                    into its old haunts, its

      the book
            coming to take its breath away
            the life   the corpse

fertile,

none of the trees

have the right

mateless

the last female

holes

skittish   circling wildly

should be

dorsal plumage

they don't ask her,

and she doesn't say

it does not go back

double knock

falsely perpetuated innocence

detailed analysis

after   paired for life,

footage of forests

of tail-wings in flight

turned to fields   in spite of

after

filmed

looking out from burrows

for perhaps thirty years

dead and decaying trees   destroyed

the inexperienced

habitats

make mistakes

she does not return

mourning

regularly
               the escape

                       orients himself with his little song

          abject   as best he can

little pigeon-sadness
                    the shock of resemblance

                       unusual whistling sound

     a picture of me looking at you   toward
                  coo
prefigures   to comfort

      looking away
        right up to the   the still life,
        human   the song itself

     make an offering of crocuses and grass

                   capturing the time before death
into danger,
      music

            skips

Canada geese

                                                                compass of spring

flock in perfect letters

                          "few men have souls so dead

                                        mosaic of brown-black
            terrestrial   tessellation

honking   dozing with white layered eyes

      soundscape   indistinguishable
      migration   from the previous years

      grey goslings are born,
      mature,
                        never die

                                                            plowed

                        the lake as dining table,
                        rough and hewn

wild swans

turn human by night

                eleven turned to swans

      enchanted and away

                              shape-shifters

and by day, trapped

gather nestle in graveyards

                weaving, she takes

                                    a lone, bitter

                a vow of silence

mute like them   a gift of four swans

                                  slowly whittles to one

            the beige fabric   with his

                                  lost pen

hollow, they   mated for life

        hold the air inside,

                                remnant of a pair   the kiss

                                does not mate again

        floating   silent

revived by stinging cloth   the bite

death by misreading

            the statues shake their heads   that which would kill you

                                    bursts into flowers

owl

at the dead end   in

branches at night

leaves   I see

here he was: up

the place

again

return

and find him gone   silently,

moth-like

the memory of the place
the place a mark

a ghost face
obscured by foliage patterns

migration

dropped its blossoms on the ground

the birds gather up
the stitches

each will know its own
scant-feathered oriole

tie the ribbons

into a wedding gown   plumage

some little plan or chart,   some
fragment from his dream

sewed it up
of

faded black and orange
human life

map
across states and seas

ragged from use

the ruby-throats
the warblers

drawn across

generations

warning

day

down to the lake

a bright false
beaches

green grass in the morning

one man walks with one dog

it is

no boats

after all
a red-winged blackbird shouting *warning*

only this:

into the cochlear

winds
cormorant formations   held above

the water like

magnets repelled

the shore an index of others:

one-page alien books
curled shining fossils
lake-broke pottery   old
jewel-like beach glass   concrete steps

darts

late night
a chickadee confused for a sparrow

path up to the

light

scruffy

cork board

de

grip

fingers press
without holding

in the traversable distance

electricity without wires

skin

lighted

quiver

a

imbedded arc of throw

fingers I

chalk the

brush
against

darting

the iridescent-tailed

score

arrows

becoming bravery

robins

                                                                              waking

               in January,

       they begin

                        awake with the first bells
                        or birds

                                      dawn song

               the refrain all day

                                                                    the long song

       I anticipate

                                            April's non-mechanical
               the years   robins

                                                          unaccompanied

                                      cycles of birds arriving and departing
               returning as different birds

golden

a memory of undulating bodies

your eyes all the time

sinking down into water carved slate pit

actual danger of falling (urban and
rural)

a memory of yellow and black birds

of wet shale fossils

on yellow and black sunflowers

draw you out

remove the tired gold orb-
soul

wash it off

the fine skull, the ardor of your brain
and in the fingers the memory

in the past, I can find you

the moss brought back in pieces
to mend itself with water

the early leaves

guessing at the warmth outside

thistles and asters;
don't fall in

house sparrows

      warm in cool summer

                                        rusty

          Djurgården macchiatos

               foraging

                    beneath our feet

the question that calls out silently
is never answered

            under blankets,

        not the stone tables,

                      but the iron tables with cut clover

               returned to Buffalo

in the bushes

                   the days we thought would not come for us

        the fat ones preen themselves

                 early warmth promising

             undelivered

              summer

Spring

memory of lace
memory of trilliums
memory of indian pipes
                    ghost-luster
                                              little blue heron
          open via two curving slits
                                                        still wild, skittish
                                              beyond range
                    different biome
                                              flushed from

                                              hunting

               to wish the impossible

          for you to see

               these specific pink-tipped daisies

bloodroot with poison ink
dimorphous bluets
yellow wort and bright verbena
spring beauty in moist open
                         present
                                        those specific irisis

               sword-like

Orpheus

the dead to life

will enter   follow   intuit

the journey   down and

to bring you   back   to formless ghosts

find a stone like a robin's

cheerily eerily   fossilized bone tissue

could cross   wooden bridge

transgressive   life's leavings

scattered seed pods

a

relief to be   *cheer cheerily*   follows

active   bursting   bubbling

against fate

desperate

the trail of music behind   issuing up

a lament

that casts such spells

can bring back

woodpecker

I'll remember

heat in the clouds

so distinct

often

rounding   third park

his red head

the light of early morning

the plight of capturing

park to park

no other local signature

in my mind   the time we have

the beginning of a long commute

I mark

a flip book of black and white

the memory of driving to work,

not the ordinary mockingbird grey

my son,

clinging to a tree

the birds,

from a forest of loss

the morning

blue jay

a third: identified by a girl

the filmic overlay of times

who could tell each blue jay apart
and had separate names for each

into a succession of captive moments

flickering

but the memories stack

mnemotechnics of madeleines

but try to think of each madeleine;

the art of poetry

together uniquely

to bring time and space

is

choose an everyday object:
anchor all related memories to it

for dear life

and to transcribe, or suggest,

that we have lost something in the translation
of time into language

the sorrow of the gap

collaboration with Lorraine

together

left out   filtering the culture

expectation to act

expansion

another poem behind this one,

a photograph of three older

crazy and alert,   female poets

before departing hold for a moment

combined differently   a rose-quartz heart

poet or artist

pixie or mother   awkward or flirtatious

excessive gestrue or

to champagne

not enough contact   to women

to birds

send a box of dresses to a friend   to little green parrotlets

to time

to go   to all sentient beings

mockingbird

rocking

the first song I sing
is not the one I remember

hush

for you

to fall asleep

repetition of

roles and music

I intone

my mother singing Brahms
every night

hush

as I fell asleep

later,

you recognize

the female quieter

the music box
knows it too

hush baby

for you

Provenance and Acknowledgements

The chapter here called "Observation" was first published as a chapbook called bird-book. The first edition of 18 poems was published in Sept. 2001 in an edition of 30. The 2nd edition of 22 poems was printed between 2002 and 2004, also in an edition of 30. The 3rd edition of 50 copies was printed in 2006 under the auspices of House Press (Buffalo). The second printing of the third edition comprised 30 copies on opaque colored cardstock in translucent vellum envelopes. Subsequent prints of the 3rd edition were unnumbered, printed on colored origami paper, and housed in translucent vellum envelopes. In 2006, bird-book was released online as a free .pdf through Armand F. Capanna's Detumescence Press; it is no longer available online.

Selections from "memory" were published as a chapbook, mnemotechnics, by above/ground press in 2013. Thank you to rob mclennan for his support as both a friend and an editor.

Selections previously appeared in *Ferrum Wheel* (1); *ixnay* (7); *N/A* (1); *name* (4/5); *Open Letters Monthly* (July 2013); *Queen Street Quarterly* (5.3); *serving suggestion* (4); *Tarpaulin Sky* (2013); Terry Cuddy's film *Transient Views of Western New York* (2001); and Monica Karwan, Brett Mastellar and Chelsea Warren's *music/dance environment, musicartmovement* (2003). Thank you to the editors, artists, readers and audiences of these works.

mnemotechnics was a Finalist for the 2012 Nightboat Poetry Prize.

Thanks to those who have been inspired to review, teach, and create art based on bird-book, including but not limited to Steven Fama for his detailed review of bird-book on *Galatea Resurrects*, Michael White for teaching bird-book to his classes at University of North Carolina at Wilmington, and Terry Cuddy, Chelsea Warren, Brett Mastellar, and Monica Karwan for their collaborative artworks. Thank you to Charles Alexander, Michelle Detorie, Gillian Devereux, Ann Fisher-Wirth, K. Lorraine Graham, Georgette Walker, Laura Hicks, Douglas Ray, Ron Silliman, Maureen Thorson, and Amish Trivedi for their support and assistance in editing the manuscript. Thanks to my parents, Pamela and Edward Smith, and my husband Nicholas McLaughlin who helped give me the time I needed to complete the second half of this book and to Paul McLaughlin for teaching me how to see as if for the first time. Thanks to Douglas Ray for bringing poetry to my everyday life and to my coven for its deep and daily emotional and artistic support.

ABOUT THE AUTHOR

Jessica Smith, Founding Editor of *Foursquare* and *name* magazines and Coven Press, serves as the Librarian for Indian Springs School, where she curates the Indian Springs School Visiting Writers Series. A native of Birmingham, Alabama, she received her B.A. in English and Comparative Literature: Language Theory, M.A. in Comparative Literature, and M.L.S. from SUNY Buffalo, where she participated in the Poetics Program. She is the author of numerous chapbooks including *Trauma Mouth* (Dusie 2015) and two full-length books of poetry, *Organic Furniture Cellar* (Outside Voices 2006) and *Life-List* (Chax 2015).

ABOUT CHAX

Founded in 1984 in Tucson, Arizona, Chax has published nearly 200 books in a variety of formats, including hand printed letterpress books and chapbooks, hybrid chapbooks, book arts editions, and trade paperback editions such as the book you are holding. In August 2014 Chax moved to Victoria, Texas, and is presented located in the University of Houston Victoria Center for the Arts. Chax is an independent 501(c)(3) organization which depends on support from various government and private funders, and, primarily, from individual donors and readers.

Recent and current books-in-progress include *The Complete Light Poems*, by Jackson Mac Low, *Andalusia*, by Susan Thackrey, *Diesel Hand*, by Nico Vassilakis, and *Dark Ladies*, by Steve McCaffery.

You may find Chax online at *http://chax.org*